UNDERSTANDING
The Bible

The Purpose And The Place

By the same author

BASIC CHRISTIANITY
YOUR CONFIRMATION
CONFESS YOUR SINS
THE EPISTLES OF JOHN: A COMMENTARY
THE CANTICLES AND SELECTED PSALMS
MEN MADE NEW
OUR GUILTY SILENCE
ONLY ONE WAY
ONE PEOPLE
CHRIST THE CONTROVERSIALIST
GUARD THE GOSPEL
BALANCED CHRISTIANITY
CHRISTIAN MISSION IN THE MODERN WORLD
BAPTISM AND FULLNESS
THE LAUSANNE COVENANT
CHRISTIAN COUNTER-CULTURE
UNDERSTANDING THE BIBLE   *Available in library*
                                 or paperback editions

OTHER BOOKS IN THIS SERIES
THE STORY OF THE OLD TESTAMENT
THE STORY OF THE NEW TESTAMENT
THE MESSAGE TO TRUST
THE BIBLE FOR TODAY

UNDERSTANDING
The Bible

The Purpose And The Place

by John R.W. Stott

Understanding the Bible

SCRIPTURE UNION

47 Marylebone Lane
London WıM 6AX

Published in the United States by
Regal Books Division, G/L Publications
Glendale, California 91209   U.S.A.

© Copyright John Stott 1978
First published in *Understanding The Bible* 1972
Reprinted 1972, 1973,
Revised 1976
First published in this form 1978

ISBN 0 85421 616 2

U.S. Library of Congress Catalog Card No. 501 7300
ISBN 0 8307 0657 7

Illustrations by Annie Valloton
Maps by Liz Leyland and Jenny Grayston

Printed in Great Britain by
McCorquodale (Newton) Ltd., Newton-le-Willows

PUBLISHER'S PREFACE

UNDERSTANDING THE BIBLE has appeared in several editions, not only in the United Kingdom, North America, Australia and India, but in such languages as German, Swedish, Dutch, Spanish, Faroese, Japanese, Chinese and Thai. The author's objectives set out in his preface are being steadily fulfilled.

Now we are issuing the original publication in five separate volumes in a further attempt to achieve those aims. We anticipate meeting an even wider need; making readily available to new readers the individual subjects on which the Rev. John R. W. Stott has written so clearly.

Their use will not be confined to the individual reader; it will be practicable to use them in study and house groups, etc.

Each book contains recommendations for further reading and an index of scripture references referred to in the text.

PREFACE

Every author owes it to the reading public to explain himself. Why has he thought fit to swell the torrent of books—especially religious books—which pours from the world's printing presses every day? Can he justify his rash enterprise? Let me at least tell you frankly the kind of people I have had in mind while writing. They fall into two categories.

First, the new Christian. With the spread of secularism in our day, an increasing number of people are being added to Christ and His Church who have no religious background whatever. Here, for example, is a young man from a non-Christian family. The Christian instruction he received at school was minimal, and possibly misleading. In any case the fashion was to pay no attention to it. He did not go to Sunday School as a kid, and he has seldom if ever been to church. But now he has found Christ, or rather been found by Him. He is told he must read the Bible daily if he is to grow into spiritual maturity. The Bible is a closed book to him, however—an unexplored, uncharted territory. Who wrote it, he asks, and when, where and why? What is its message? What is the foundation for its claim to be a 'holy' or special book, the book of God? And how is it to be read and interpreted? These are proper questions to ask, and some answer must be given to them before the new Christian can derive maximum benefit from his Bible reading.

Then, secondly, there is the Christian of several years' standing. In the main, he has been a conscientious Bible reader. He has read his portion faithfully every day. But somehow it has become a stale habit. The years have passed, and he himself has changed and matured as a person. Yet he has not developed as a Christian in any comparable way. A sign (and cause) of this is that he still reads the Bible as he did when he was a child, or a new convert. Now he is tired of his superficiality, his immaturity, and not a little ashamed. He longs to become an adult, integrated Christian, who knows and pleases God, fulfils himself in serving others and can commend the gospel in meaningful terms to a lost, bewildered generation.

My desire is to assure such a Christian that the secrets of Christian maturity are ready to be found in Scripture by all who seek them. There is a breadth to God's Word which few of us ever encompass, a depth which we seldom plumb.

In particular, our Christianity is mean because our Christ is mean. We impoverish ourselves by our low and paltry views of Him. Some speak of Him today as if He were a kind of syringe to be carried about in our pocket, so that when we are feeling depressed we can give ourselves a fix and take a trip into fantasy. But Christ cannot be used or manipulated like that. The contemporary Church seems to have little understanding of the greatness of Jesus Christ as lord of creation and lord of the Church, before whom our place is on our faces in the dust. Nor do we seem to see His victory as the New Testament portrays it, with all things under His feet, so that if we are joined to Christ, all things are under our feet as well.

It seems to me that our greatest need today is an enlarged vision of Jesus Christ. We need to see Him as the One in whom alone the fulness of God dwells and in whom alone we can come to fulness of life.[1]

There is only one way to gain clear, true, fresh, lofty views of Christ, and that is through the Bible. The Bible is the prism by which the light of Jesus Christ is broken into its many and beautiful colours. The Bible is the portrait of Jesus Christ. We need to gaze upon Him with such intensity of desire that (by the gracious work of the Holy Spirit) He comes alive to us, meets with us, and fills us with Himself.

In order to apprehend Jesus Christ in His fulness, it is essential to understand the setting within which God offers Him to us. God gave Christ to the world in a specific geographical, historical and theological context. More simply, He sent Him to a particular place (Palestine), at a particular time (the climax of centuries of Jewish history) and within a particular framework of truth (progressively revealed and permanently recorded in the Bible). So the following chapters are concerned with the geography, history, theology, authority and interpretation of the Bible. Their object is to present the setting within which God once revealed and now offers Christ, so that we may the better grasp for ourselves and share with others the glorious fulness of Jesus Christ Himself.

NOTE

1 See Col. 1.19; 2.9, 10

THE PURPOSE AND THE PLACE

The choice of a book to read and the way in which we read it are determined largely by the author's purpose in writing it. Is it a textbook of science or history intended to inform, or a novel meant purely to entertain? Is it a piece of serious prose or poetry in which the writer reflects on life and stimulates the reader to think about it too? Does it speak in any meaningful way to the contemporary world? Or is it perhaps a controversial work in which he deliberately sets out to argue his point of view? Moreover, is the author qualified to write on his subject? It is questions like these which are in our minds when we ask 'Is it worth reading?'

Most books supply the prospective reader with the information he wants about who wrote them and why. Either the author tells us candidly in a Preface about himself and his object in writing, or the publisher does so in the 'blurb' on the dust cover. Most readers spend time

1

examining these before committing themselves to buy, borrow or read the book.

It is a great pity that readers of the Bible do not always pursue the same enquiries. Many appear to pick it up and begin their reading at random. Or they start at Genesis and get stuck in Leviticus. Or they may doggedly persevere from a sense of duty, even reading the whole Bible through section by section in five years, but without deriving much benefit from their study because they lack understanding of the book's overall purpose. Or indeed they may give up Bible reading, or never start it, because they cannot see how the tale of a far-away people in a far-away age could have any relevance for them today.

In any case, how can the Bible, which in fact is not a book but a library of sixty-six books, possibly be said to have a 'purpose'? Was it not compiled by different authors at different times with different objectives? Yes and no. There is indeed a wide variety of human author and theme. Yet behind these, Christians believe, there lies a single divine Author with a single unifying theme.

What this theme is the Bible itself declares. It is stated several times in several places, but perhaps nowhere more succinctly than by the Apostle Paul to Timothy:

> 'From childhood you have been acquainted with the sacred writings which are able to instruct you for salvation through faith in Christ Jesus. All Scripture is inspired by God and profitable for teaching, for reproof, for correction, and for training in righteousness, that the man of God may be complete, equipped for every good work.'[1]

Here the apostle brings together both the origin and the object of Scripture, where it comes from and what it is intended for. Its origin: 'inspired by God'. Its object: 'profitable' for men. Indeed, it is profitable for men only because it is inspired by God. The subject of Biblical

2

inspiration I must leave for another occasion; in this book I want to investigate the nature of the Bible's profitability. For this I will take up three words which Paul used—'salvation', 'Christ' and 'faith'.

A Book of Salvation

Perhaps no Biblical word has suffered more from misuse and misunderstanding than the word 'salvation'. Some of us Christians are to blame for the caricature of it which we have presented to the world. As a result, 'salvation' has become for many a source of embarrassment, even an object of ridicule. We need to rescue it from the narrow concept to which we have often debased it. For 'salvation' is a big and noble word, as I shall soon elaborate. Salvation is freedom. Yes, and renewal too; ultimately the renewal of the whole cosmos.

Now the supreme purpose of the Bible, Paul writes to Timothy, is to instruct its readers 'for salvation'. This immediately indicates that Scripture has a practical purpose, and that this purpose is moral rather than intellectual. Or rather its intellectual instruction (its 'wisdom', as the Greek word implies) is given with a view to the moral experience called 'salvation'.

In order to grasp more firmly this positive purpose of Scripture, it may be helpful to contrast it with some negatives.

First, the purpose of the Bible is not scientific. This is not to say that the teaching of Scripture and of science are in conflict with one another for, when we keep each to its proper sphere, they are not. Indeed, if the God of truth is the author of both, they could not be. Nor is it to say that the two spheres never overlap and that nothing in the Bible partakes of the nature of science, for the Bible does contain statements of fact which can be (and in many cases have been) scientifically verified. For example, a number of historical facts are recorded, such as that Nebuchadrezzar King of Babylon besieged, took and virtually destroyed Jerusalem, and that Jesus of Nazareth was born when Augustus was Emperor of Rome. What I am rather asserting is that, though the Bible may contain some science, the *purpose* of the Bible is not scientific.

Science (or at least natural science) is a body of knowledge painstakingly acquired by observation, experiment and induction. The purpose of God through Scripture, however, has been to disclose truths which could not be discovered by this empirical method, but would have remained unknown and undiscovered if He had not revealed them. For instance, science may be able to tell us something about man's physical origins (even this is an open question); only the Bible reveals man's nature, both his unique nobility as a creature made in the Creator's image and his degradation as a self-centred sinner in revolt against his Creator.

Next, the purpose of the Bible is not literary. Some years ago a book was published entitled *The Bible Designed to be read as Literature*. It was beautifully produced. Versification was abandoned. And the lay-out indicated plainly what was poetry and what prose. All this was helpful. Further, no one can deny, whatever his beliefs or disbeliefs, that the Bible does contain noble literature. It treats the great themes of human life and destiny, and handles them with simplicity, insight and imagination. So fine is the translation in some countries that the Bible has become part of the nation's literary heritage. Nevertheless, God did not design the Bible as great literature. It contains some glaring stylistic weaknesses. The New Testament was largely written in *koine* Greek, the everyday language of market and office, and much of it lacks literary polish, even grammatical accuracy. The purpose of the Bible is to be found in its message, not its style.

Thirdly, the purpose of the Bible is not philosophical. Of course Scripture contains profound wisdom, in fact the wisdom of God. But some of the great themes with which philosophers have always wrestled are not given a thorough treatment in Scripture. Take the great problems of suffering and evil. As phenomena of human experience they figure prominently throughout the Bible. On almost every page men sin and men suffer. And some light is thrown—supremely by the cross—on both problems. But no ultimate solution to either is offered, nor are the ways of God justified in relation to them. Even in the Book of Job, which concentrates on the problem of suffering, Job in the end humbles himself before God without understanding God's providence. I think the reason is simply that the Bible is more a practical than a theoretical book. It is more concerned to tell us how to bear suffering and overcome evil than it is to philosophize about their origin and purpose.

So the Bible is primarily a book neither of science, nor of literature, nor of philosophy, but of salvation.

In saying this we must give the word 'salvation' its broadest possible meaning. Salvation is far more than the forgiveness of sins. It includes the whole sweep of God's purpose to redeem and restore mankind, and indeed all creation. What we claim for the Bible is that it unfolds God's total plan.

It begins with the creation, so that we may know the divine likeness in which we were made, the obligations which we have repudiated and the heights from which we have fallen. We can understand neither what we are in sin nor what we may be by grace until we know what we once were by creation.

The Bible goes on to tell us how sin entered into the world, and death as a result of sin. It emphasizes the gravity of sin as a revolt against the authority of God our Creator and Lord, and the justice of His judgment upon

5

it. There are many salutary warnings in Scripture about the perils of disobedience.

But the main thrust is always that God loves the very rebels who deserve nothing at His hand but judgment. Before time began, Scripture says, His plan of salvation took shape. It originated in His grace, His free and unmerited mercy. He made with Abraham a covenant of grace, promising through his posterity to bless all the families of the earth. The rest of the Old Testament is devoted to an account of His gracious dealings with Abraham's posterity, the people of Israel. In spite of their obstinate rejection of His word, as it came to them through law and prophets, He never cast them off. *They* broke the covenant, not He.

The historical coming of Jesus Christ was in fulfilment of His covenant:

'Blessed be the Lord God of Israel,
for He has visited and redeemed His people,
and has raised up a horn of salvation for us
in the house of His servant David,
as He spoke by the mouth of His holy prophets
    from of old,
that we should be saved from our enemies,
and from the hand of all who hate us;
to perform the mercy promised to our fathers,
and to remember His holy covenant,
the oath which He swore to our father Abraham, to
    grant us
that we, being delivered from the hand of our enemies,
might serve Him without fear,
in holiness and righteousness before Him all the days
    of our life.'[2]

It is important to observe that the promised 'salvation' from 'our enemies' is understood in terms of 'holiness and righteousness' and—later in the *Benedictus*—of 'the forgiveness of their sins through the tender mercy of our God'.

So the New Testament concentrates on the outworking of this salvation, on the way of 'forgiveness' and of 'holiness' through Jesus Christ's death, resurrection and gift of the Spirit. The apostles emphasize that forgiveness is possible only through the sin-bearing death of Christ, and a new birth leading to a new life only through the Spirit of Christ. Then the epistles are full of practical ethical instruction. As the NEB renders 2 Timothy 3.16, Scripture is profitable not only 'for teaching the truth and refuting error' but 'for reformation of manners and discipline in right living'. It also portrays Christ's Church as the society of the saved, who are called to a life of sacrificial service and witness in the world.

Finally, the New Testament authors insist that although God's people have already in one sense been saved, in another their salvation lies still in the future. We are given the promise that one day our bodies will be redeemed. 'In this hope we were saved.'[3] And in this final redemption the whole creation will somehow be involved. If we are to be clothed with new bodies, there is also going to be a new heaven and a new earth pervaded by righteousness alone. Then and only then, with no sin either in our nature or in our society, will God's salvation be complete. The glorious liberty of God's children will be the freedom to serve. God will be everything to everybody.[4]

Such is the comprehensive salvation set forth in Scripture. Conceived in a past eternity, achieved at a point in time and historically worked out in human experience, it will reach its consummation in the eternity of the future. The Bible is unique in its claim to instruct us for 'such a great salvation.'[5]

The salvation for which the Bible instructs us is available 'through faith in Christ Jesus'. Therefore, since Scripture concerns salvation and salvation is through Christ, Scripture is full of Christ.

Jesus Himself thus understood the nature and function of the Bible. 'The Scriptures,' He said, 'bear witness to Me.'[6] Again, walking with two disciples after the Resurrection from Jerusalem to Emmaus, He rebuked them for their folly and unbelief, due to their ignorance of Scripture. Luke who tells the story adds:

> 'And beginning with Moses and all the prophets, He interpreted to them in all the scriptures the things concerning Himself.'[7]

A little while later the risen Lord said to a wider group of His followers:

> 'These are My words which I spoke to you, while I was still with you, that everything written about Me in the law of Moses and the prophets and the psalms must be fulfilled.'[8]

Christ's assertion was, then, not only that the Scriptures bore witness to Him in a general way but that in each of the three divisions of Old Testament Scripture—the law, the prophets and the psalms (or 'writings')—there were things concerning Him, and that all these things must be fulfilled.

The fundamental relation between the Old Testament and the New Testament, according to Christ, is that between promise and fulfilment. The very first word Jesus uttered in His public ministry (in the Greek text of the Gospel of Mark) indicates this. It was the word 'fulfilled':

'The time is fulfilled, and the kingdom of God is at hand; repent, and believe in the gospel.'[9]

Jesus Christ was deeply convinced that the long centuries of expectation were over, and that He Himself had ushered in the days of fulfilment. So He could say to His apostles:

'Blessed are your eyes, for they see, and your ears, for they hear. Truly, I say to you, many prophets and righteous men longed to see what you see, and did not see it, and to hear what you hear, and did not hear it.'[10]

In the light of this claim, we shall look first at the Old Testament in its three divisions, then at the New Testament, and try to see how our Saviour Jesus Christ Himself (in terms of promise and fulfilment) is Scripture's uniting theme.

By the 'law' was meant the Pentateuch, the first five books of the Old Testament. Can we really find Christ in them? Yes indeed.

To begin with, they contain some foundation prophecies of God's salvation through Christ, which underlie the rest of the Bible. God promised first that the seed of Eve would bruise the serpent's head, next that through Abraham's posterity He would bless all the families of the earth, and later that 'the sceptre shall not depart from Judah . . . until He comes to whom it belongs', whom the people will obey.[11] Thus it was revealed—already in the first book of the Bible—that the Messiah would be human (descended from Eve) and Jewish (descended from Abraham and of the tribe of Judah), and that He would crush Satan, bless the world and rule as king for ever.

Another important prophecy of Christ in the law represents Him as being Himself the perfect Prophet. Moses said to the people:

9

'The Lord your God will raise up for you a Prophet like me from among you, from your brethren—Him you shall heed— . . . and I will put My words in His mouth, and He shall speak to them all that I command Him'.[12]

It was not only by direct prophecies that the law pointed forward to Christ, but also by more indirect pictures. In it the Messiah was foreshadowed as well as foretold. Indeed, God's dealings with Israel in choosing them, redeeming them, establishing His covenant with them, making atonement for their sins through sacrifice, and causing them to inherit the land of Canaan all set forth in limited and national terms what would one day be available to all men through Christ. Christians can say today: God has chosen us in Christ and made us a people for His own possession. Christ shed His blood to atone for our sins and ratify the new covenant. He has redeemed us not from Egyptian bondage but from the bondage of sin. He is our great high priest who offered Himself on the cross, as one sacrifice for sins for ever, and all priesthood and sacrifice are fulfilled in Him. Further, by His resurrection we have been born again to a living hope, 'to an inheritance which is imperishable, undefiled and unfading' and is reserved in heaven for us.[13] These great Christian words, which portray various aspects of our salvation through Christ—election, atonement, covenant, redemption, sacrifice, inheritance—all began to be used in the Old Testament of God's grace towards Israel.

There is yet a third way in which the law bears witness to Christ. It is elaborated by the apostle Paul in his Galatian letter:

'Now before faith came, we were confined under the law, kept under restraint until faith should be revealed. So that the law was our custodian until Christ came, that we might be justified by faith.'[14]

The law is vividly portrayed by the Greek words Paul used as a military garrison hemming us in ('confined'), a gaoler keeping us under lock and key ('under restraint') and a tutor charged with the discipline of minors ('our custodian'). All this is because the moral law condemned the lawbreaker without in itself offering any remedy. In this way it pointed to Christ. Its very condemnation made Christ necessary. It held us in bondage 'until Christ came', who alone could set us free. We are condemned by the law, but justified through faith in Christ.

Christ in the Prophets

As we turn now from the law to the prophets, we need to remember that the Old Testament division known as 'the prophets' included the history books (Joshua, Judges, Samuel and Kings) as 'the former prophets' because the authors were judged to have written prophetic or sacred history, as well as 'the latter prophets' whom we call the major and minor prophets.

Many readers of the Bible have found the history of Israel extremely tedious and cannot imagine how all those dreary kings could have anything to do with Christ! When we remember, however, that Christ's first words about 'the time is fulfilled' immediately led on to 'the kingdom of God has drawn near', we have in the word 'kingdom' the clue we need. Israel began as a 'theocracy', a nation under the direct rule of God. Even when the people rejected the divine rule by demanding a king like the other nations and God granted their request, they knew that ultimately He continued to be their King, for they continued to be His people, and that their kings reigned as it were as His viceroys.

Nevertheless, the rule of the kings, of both the northern kingdom Israel and the southern kingdom Judah, left much to be desired. The monarchy was marred now

11

externally by foreign wars, now internally by injustice and oppression. Both kingdoms also had the instability of all human institutions, as kings acceded to the throne and prospered and died. And sometimes they shrank to tiny territories as their land was overrun by invading armies, until in the end both capitals were taken and both nations suffered a humiliating exile. It is not surprising that God used their experience of the unsatisfactoriness of human rule to clarify their understanding of the perfections of the future Messianic kingdom and to strengthen their longing for it.

Already God had made a covenant with King David to build him a house and through his posterity to establish his throne for ever.[15] Now the prophets began to describe what kind of king this 'son of David' would be. They were clear that He would embody the ideals of kingship which the kings of Israel and Judah, and even David himself, so imperfectly foreshadowed. In His kingdom oppression would give place to justice, and war to peace. And there would be no limit to either its extent or its duration. For His dominion would stretch from sea to sea, even to the ends of the earth, and would last for ever. These four characteristics of the kingdom of the Messiah —peace, justice, universality and eternity—are brought together in one of Isaiah's most famous prophecies:

'For unto us a child is born, to us a son is given;
  and the government will be upon His shoulder, and His
    name will be called
  "Wonderful Counsellor, Mighty God, Everlasting
    Father, Prince of Peace."
Of the increase of his government and of peace there
    will be no end,
upon the throne of David, and over His kingdom,
  to establish it, and to uphold it
with justice and with righteousness

12

from this time forth and for evermore.
The zeal of the Lord of hosts will do this.'[16]

If the prophets foretold the glory of the Messiah, they foretold His sufferings also. The best-known such prophecy, obviously definitive for our Lord's own understanding of His ministry, is that of the suffering servant in Isaiah 53. He would be 'despised and rejected of men, a man of sorrows, and acquainted with grief'. Above all, He would bear his people's sins:

'He was wounded for our transgressions,
    He was bruised for our iniquities;
upon Him was the chastisement that made us whole,
    and with His stripes we are healed.
All we like sheep have gone astray;
    we have turned every one to his own way;
    and the Lord has laid on Him the iniquity of us all.'[17]

Christ in the Writings

The third division of the Old Testament was 'the writings', sometimes called 'the psalms' because the Psalter was the chief book of this section. Several psalms are applied to Jesus Christ in the New Testament, psalms which include references to His deity, humanity, sufferings and exaltation. Thus the words 'You are My son, today I have begotten You'[18] were used (at least in part) by God the Father in direct address to His Son at both His baptism and His transfiguration. The allusions in Psalm 8 to man as 'made a little lower than the angels' and 'crowned with glory and honour', are applied to Christ by the author of the Letter to the Hebrews. Jesus Himself quoted Ps. 22.1 from the cross 'My God, My God, why hast Thou forsaken Me?', claiming that He had personally experienced and fulfilled the terrible God-

13

forsakenness which the psalmist expressed. He also quoted David's saying in Ps. 110.1 'The Lord says to my Lord: "Sit at My right hand, till I make Your enemies Your footstool"', and asked His critics how in their view the Messiah could be both David's Lord and David's son.

'The writings' contain, in addition, what is often called the wisdom literature of the Old Testament. The 'wise men' appear to have become a distinct group in Israel during the later period of the monarchy, alongside the prophets and the priests. They knew that the beginning of wisdom was to fear God and depart from evil. Often they extolled wisdom in glowing terms, as more precious than gold, silver and jewels, and occasionally they appeared even to personify wisdom as the agent of God's creation:

'When He established the heavens, I was there,
    when He drew a circle on the face of the deep,
when He assigned to the sea its limit, so that the waters
    might not transgress His command,
when He marked out the foundations of the earth,
then I was beside Him, like a master workman;
and I was daily His delight, rejoicing before Him
    always,
rejoicing in His inhabited world
    and delighting in the sons of men.'[19]

Christians have no difficulty in recognizing that this wisdom of God is uniquely incorporated in Jesus Christ, the personal 'Word' who was in the beginning with God and through whom all things were made.[20]

The Old Testament expectation of Christ—in the law, the prophets and the writings—is seen to have been extremely diverse. Jesus Himself summed it up in the comprehensive expression that 'the Christ should suffer . . . and enter into His glory'.[21] The apostle Peter took up the phrase, conceding that the prophets did not fully

14

understand 'what person or time was indicated by the Spirit of Christ within them when predicting the sufferings of Christ and the subsequent glory'.[22] But this double strand of prophecy was there, representing Him as the priest who would offer Himself as a sacrifice for sin and the king whose glorious reign would know no end.

In fact, another way of summing up the Old Testament witness to Christ is to say that it depicts Him as a prophet greater than Moses, a priest greater than Aaron and a king greater than David. That is to say, He will perfectly reveal God to man, reconcile man to God and rule over man for God. In Him the Old Testament ideals of prophecy, priesthood and kingship will find their final fulfilment.

Christ in the New Testament

If the idea of discovering Christ in the Old Testament seems at first sight strange, there is no similar difficulty about finding Him in the New. The gospels tell the story from different points of view of the birth, life, death and ressurection of Jesus, and supply a sample of His words and works.

These 'memoirs of the apostles', as they used to be called in the early church, came rightly to be known as 'Gospels', for each evangelist tells his story as 'gospel' or good news of Christ and His salvation. They do not present Him as a biographer might. For they are essentially witnesses, directing their readers' attention to one they believed to be the God-man, born to save His people from their sins, whose words were words of eternal life, whose works dramatized the glory of His kingdom, who died as a ransom for sinners and rose in triumph to be Lord of all.

You might suppose that the Acts of the Apostles, which tells the story of the early days of Christianity, is more about the church than about Christ. Yet this would grievously misrepresent its nature. Luke its author is of a different persuasion. In introducing his work to Theophilus (for whom he is writing) he describes his first book (the Gospel of Luke) as containing 'all that Jesus began both to do and teach'. The implication is that the Acts story will contain all that Jesus *continued* to do and teach through His apostles. So in the Acts we listen to Christ as He was still speaking to men, though now through the great sermons of the apostles Peter and Paul which Luke records. We also see the miracles which He did through them, for 'many wonders and signs were done *through* the apostles' by Christ.[23] And we watch Christ building His own church by adding converts to it:

'And the Lord added to their number day by day those who were being saved.'[24]

The epistles extend the New Testament's witness to Christ by unfolding further the glory of His divine-human person and saving work, and by relating the life of the Christian and of the church to Him. The apostles exalt Christ as the one in whom 'all the fulness of God was pleased to dwell' and through whom we ourselves come to 'fulness of life'.[25] In Christ God has 'blessed us . . . with every spiritual blessing', they say,[26] so that we can do all things through Him who inwardly strengthens us.[27] The Christ the apostles present is an all-sufficient Christ, who is able to save to the uttermost and for all time 'those who draw near to God through Him'.[28]

The Bible's disclosure of Christ reaches its climax in the Revelation of John. He is portrayed in the vivid imagery which characterizes this book. First He appears as a glorified man 'in the midst of the lampstands'. These represent the churches, which the risen Christ is seen to patrol and superintend, so that He is able to say to each 'I know your works.'[29] Then the scene changes from

16

earth to heaven, and Jesus Christ appears in the guise of 'a Lamb . . . , as though it had been slain'. The countless international crowd of the redeemed are even said to have 'washed their robes and made them white in the blood of the Lamb', which means that they owe their righteousness to Christ crucified alone.[30] Then towards the end of the book Christ is seen as a majestic rider on a white horse, going forth to judgment, with His name inscribed upon him 'King of kings and Lord of lords'.[31] Finally we are introduced to Him as the Heavenly Bridegroom for, we are told, 'the marriage of the Lamb has come, and his Bride has made herself ready'. His bride is the glorified Church which is then seen 'coming down out of heaven from God, prepared as a bride adorned for her husband'.[32] Almost the last words of the Revelation are 'The Spirit and the Bride say, "Come". And let him who hears say, "Come" . . . Come, Lord Jesus!'[33]

There is great diversity of content, style and purpose among the books of the Bible, and in some books the witness to Christ is indirect, even oblique. But this brief survey of the Old and New Testaments should be enough to demonstrate that 'the testimony of Jesus is the spirit of prophecy'.[34] If we want to know Christ and His salvation, it is to the Bible we must turn. For the Bible is God's own portrait of Christ. We can never know Him otherwise. As Jerome put it in the fourth century A.D., 'Ignorance of the Scriptures is ignorance of Christ'.[35]

Just as in a children's treasure hunt, one is sometimes fortunate enough to stumble immediately upon the treasure but usually has to follow laboriously from clue to clue until at last the treasure is found, so it is with Bible reading. Some verses point one direct to Christ. Others are remote clues. But a painstaking pursuit of the clues will ultimately lead every reader to that treasure whose worth is beyond price.

Through Faith

The Scriptures are able to instruct us for salvation, the apostle Paul wrote, 'through faith in Christ Jesus'. Since their purpose (or the purpose of the divine author through them) is to bring us to salvation, and since salvation is in Christ, they point us to Christ, as we have seen. But their object in pointing us to Christ is not simply that we should know about Him and understand Him, nor even that we should admire Him, but that we should put our trust in Him. Scripture bears witness to Christ not in order to satisfy our curiosity but in order to elicit our faith.

There is much misunderstanding about faith. It is commonly supposed to be a leap in the dark, totally incompatible with reason. This is not so. True faith is never unreasonable, because its object is always trustworthy. When we human beings trust one another, the reasonableness of our trust depends on the relative trustworthiness of the people concerned. But the Bible bears witness to Jesus Christ as absolutely trustworthy. It tells us who He is and what He has done, and the evidence it supplies for His unique person and work is extremely compelling. As we expose ourselves to the biblical witness to this Christ and as we feel its impact—profound yet simple, varied yet unanimous—God creates faith within us. We receive the testimony. We believe.

This is what Paul meant when he wrote:

'So faith comes from what is heard, and what is heard comes by the preaching of Christ'.[36]

We have seen that God's purpose in and through the Bible is severely practical. He has ordained it as His chief instrument for bringing men to 'salvation', understood in its widest and fullest sense. The whole Bible is a gospel of salvation, and the gospel is 'the power of God for

18

salvation to every one who has faith'.[37] So it points its many fingers unerringly to Christ, so that its readers will see Him, believe in Him and be saved.

The apostle John writes something very similar at the end of his Gospel. He has recorded only a selection of the signs of Jesus, he says, for Jesus performed many others. He goes on:

'But these are written that you may believe that Jesus is the Christ, the Son of God, and that believing you may have life in His name'.[38]

John sees the ultimate purpose of Scripture ('what is written') just as Paul sees it. John calls it 'life', Paul 'salvation', but the words are virtually synonymous. Both apostles are further agreed that this life or salvation is in Christ, and that to receive it we must believe in Him. The sequence, Scripture—Christ—faith—salvation, is exactly the same. Scripture testifies to Christ in order to evoke faith in Christ, in order to bring life to the believer.

The conclusion is simple. Whenever we read the Bible, we must look for Christ. And we must go on looking until we see and so believe. Only as we continue to appropriate by faith the riches of Christ which are disclosed to us in Scripture shall we grow into spiritual maturity, and become men and women of God who are 'complete, equipped for every good work'.

For Further Reading

The Lion Handbook to the Bible (Lion Publishing 1973, 680 pages). A comprehensive guide to all the books of the Bible, together with 437 pictures, 68 maps, 20 charts and 60 specialist articles. An exciting reference book, written by trustworthy scholars, which will prove a continuing mine of helpful information.

Every Man a Bible Student by J. E. Church (Paternoster 1976, 126 pages). An elementary handbook for basic Bible Study for those who want to live their faith as well as learn about it. The author, a doctor and missionary intimately connected with the East African revival, handles 47 subjects including the main biblical doctrines and such practical matters as temptation, compromise, apostasy and the problem of pain.

NOTES

1 2 Tim. 3.15–17
2 Luke 1.68–75
3 Rom. 8.24
4 Rom. 8.21; 1 Cor. 15.28
5 Heb. 2.3
6 John 5.39
7 Lk. 24.27
8 Lk. 24.44
9 Mk. 1.15
10 Mt. 13.16, 17
11 Gen. 3.15; 12.3; 49.10
12 Deut. 18.15, 18b
13 1 Pet. 1.3, 4
14 Gal. 3.23, 24
15 2 Sam. 7.8–17
16 Is. 9.6, 7
17 Is. 53.5, 6
18 Ps. 2.7
19 Prov. 8.27–31
20 see Jn. 1.1–3; Col. 2.3
21 Lk. 24.26
22 1 Pet. 1.11

23 Acts 2.43
24 Acts 2.47
25 Col. 1.19; 2.9, 10
26 Eph. 1.3
27 Phil. 4.13
28 Heb. 7.25
29 Rev. 1–3
30 Rev. 5.6; 7.14
31 Rev. 19.11–16
32 see Rev. 19.7–9; 21.2
33 Rev. 22.17, 20
34 Rev. 19.10
35 In the prologue to his commentary on Isaiah, quoted in Vatican II's *Dogmatic Constitution on Divine Revelation*, para. 25
36 Rom. 10.17
37 Rom. 1.16
38 Jn. 20.31

THE LAND OF THE BIBLE

God's purpose to call out from the world a people for Himself began to unfold in a particular part of the world's surface and during a particular period of the world's history. It is not possible to understand its meaning, therefore, without some knowledge of its historical and geographical setting.

Yet the very mention of history and geography, especially Bible history and Bible geography, is enough to switch some people off. They shudder as they recall boring RE lessons at school, with date-lists of dreary Israelite kings to memorize and Paul's interminable missionary journeys to plot on a map. If you feel like that, I sympathize with you. I suffered that way too. So evidently did the theological student who was required in an exam to distinguish between the prophets Elijah and Elisha. As he did not have the foggiest notion which was which, it is rumoured that his essay began: 'Let us not haggle over the differences between these two truly great

The Fertile Crescent

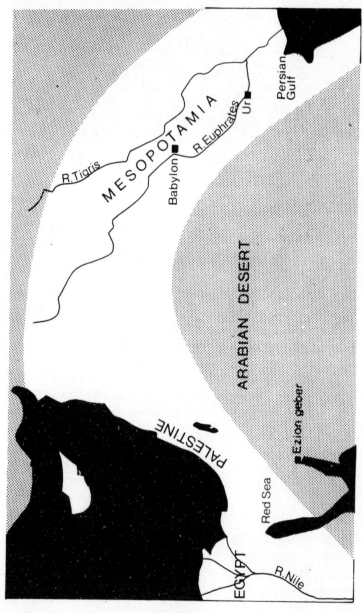

men. But let us rather give a list of the kings of Israel and Judah in their chronological order.'

Some folk who have no taste for either history or geography may ask rather impatiently why God did not give us instead a simple set of dogmas to believe and rules to obey. Why did He have to reveal Himself in a rather remote historical and geographical context, so that we have to struggle to understand the context before we can grasp the revelation? One reply might be: 'Because God chose to do it that way' and 'Stop asking impertinent questions.' But the questions are perfectly proper ones.

A better answer would be that the living God is a personal God, who made us as persons in His own image and insists on treating as persons the persons He has made. So the whole process of revelation has been the self-disclosure of a Person to persons, to real persons like ourselves who actually lived in a certain place at a certain time. In saying this, I am not denying that God has revealed His truth in words. I am rather asserting that His revelation has been 'personal' and 'propositional' at one and the same time. That is, the truths He has revealed have not descended from heaven by parachute. They have not appeared in disjointed form as 'The Thoughts of God', comparable to Chairman Mao's. They have rather been made known in and through the living experience of human beings, culminating in His own Son, the Word made flesh.

Moreover, if God had simply supplied us with a systematic catalogue of dos and don'ts for everyday belief and behaviour, it would have been far too abstract to be useful. And if it had been expressed in the idiom of one age or generation, it would have been largely meaningless to others. But as it is, God revealed Himself in personal situations, which being human are concrete and readily intelligible in every generation. Their record in Scripture enables us to 'see' for ourselves.

God's dealings with the nation of Israel and with individuals are recorded, we are told, 'for our instruction'.[1] And the instruction they give consists of both encouragement and warning.

'The encouragement of the Scriptures'[2] is tremendous. Even the great men of the Biblical story, it is emphasized, were 'of like nature' with us.[3] Yet we watch them overcoming in their struggle with temptation and doubt; refusing to bow down to idols and willing to accept death rather than compromise their allegiance to the living God; believing the promises of God in spite of every evidence to the contrary; standing alone in an age of prevailing apostasy; loving and serving their own generation; and bravely bearing witness to the truth.

Scripture contains warning as well as encouragement, for it refuses to conceal the faults even of its great men. It tells us frankly how righteous Noah got drunk; how once Abraham, the giant of faith, fell so deeply into unbelief that he was ready even to expose his wife to moral danger in order to save his own skin; how Jacob schemed and Joseph boasted; how Moses, the meekest man on earth, lost his temper; how David, who found favour in the sight of God, yet committed theft, murder and adultery in a single surrender to passion; how Job, 'blameless and upright, one who feared God and turned away from evil', yet, under the provocation of great adversity, cried out in bitterness and cursed the day of his birth; and how the whole nation of Israel, despite its many unique privileges, broke the covenant of God. The Bible is equally candid with its New Testament characters. They too were men of flesh and blood like us, who gave way sometimes to unbelief, compromise, boastfulness, indiscipline and disobedience. 'Now these things are warnings to us'[4]

God wants to deal with us in our situation of time and place, as He dealt with the Biblical characters in theirs.

So to understand His ways with us, we must understand His ways with them. And to understand this, we must know something of both where and when it all happened. We must be able to visualize it. For this history and this geography constitute the arena in which God chose uniuely to speak and to act.

It used to be seriously argued by Christian geographers in the middle ages that Jerusalem was the centre of the earth. Their maps illustrated their belief. And in the ancient Church of the Holy Sepulchre in Jerusalem (which is built over the supposed site of the crucifixion and resurrection of Jesus) a stone is let into the floor to mark what was thought to be the precise spot.

Of course this is sheer nonsense, geographically speaking. Theologically, however, Christians would defend it as true. To them Palestine is 'the Holy Land', a region distinct from all others. It is also the centre of the world's history and geography in this sense that here lay 'the promised land' which God pledged to Abraham some two thousand years before Christ; here the Saviour of the world both lived and died; and here the Christian mission was born, which was to outlive the Roman empire and change the course of world history.

Further, Christians believe in the providence of God. We cannot therefore imagine that the choice of Palestine as the stage for the drama of salvation was an accident. One of its obvious features is that it acts as a kind of bridge between three continents. Europe, Asia and Africa converge at the eastern seaboard of the Mediterranean, and their citizens have ever mingled with each other on its trade routes by sea and land. Consequently, not only has Palestine been invaded and subjugated by armies from all three—first Egyptian, then Assyrian, Babylonian and Persian, and finally Greek and Roman—but it became an admirable springboard for spiritual counter-attack, the soldiers of Jesus Christ marching north, south, east and west to the conquest of the world. 'You shall be My witnesses,' His last words to them had been, 'in Jerusalem and in all Judea and Samaria and to the end of the earth'.[5] Strategically, therefore, God had set Jerusalem 'in the centre of the nations'.[6] If Christ's witnesses had taught more clearly the middle eastern origins of Christianity, one wonders if the gospel would ever have become so closely associated in the minds of Africans and Asians with the white and the western world.

'Palestine'—the word came originally from the Philistines who occupied a small south western section of it— is itself only a part of the arena of Old Testament history. The wider scene has often been called the 'Fertile Crescent', because it sweeps round in a semi-circle from Egypt to Mesopotamia, from the Nile valley to the alluvial plain watered by the Euphrates and Tigris rivers, enclosing the arid Arabian desert. In order to understand the history of God's people, one needs to keep this crescent in mind, and not least the two great rivers which form its extremities. For God called Abraham from Ur of the Chaldees, situated only nine miles from the River Euphrates in Southern Iraq, and Moses from Egypt where he had narrowly escaped drowning as a baby in the River Nile. The very words 'Egypt' and 'Babylonia' reminded Israelites of the saving initiatives of their God, for these countries were the scenes of their two bitter captivities, from which their God had delivered them.

Palestine

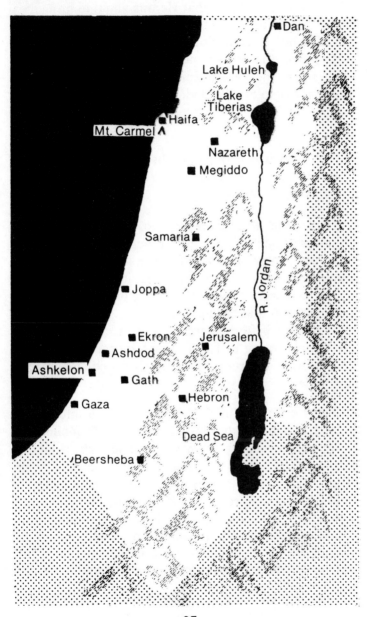

- Dan
- Lake Huleh
- Lake Tiberias
- Haifa
- Mt. Carmel ∧
- Nazareth
- Megiddo
- Samaria
- Joppa
- R. Jordan
- Ekron
- Jerusalem
- Ashdod
- Ashkelon
- Gath
- Gaza
- Hebron
- Dead Sea
- Beersheba

A Good Land

When God told Moses that He was about to bring them out of Egypt into Canaan, He described it as 'a good and broad land, a land flowing with milk and honey',[7] adding later that it was 'the most glorious of all lands'.[8] And when the twelve spies reported, whom Moses had sent to explore the land, they confirmed this description from their own experience. Joshua and Caleb said:

'The land, which we passed through to spy it out, is an exceedingly good land . . ., a land which flows with milk and honey'.[9]

They were able, moreover, to supply evidence for their assertion, for they had brought back with them from the Valley of Eshcol (a little north of Hebron) a single cluster of grapes so heavy that it had to be slung on a pole and carried by two of them, together with some pomegranates and figs as well.[10]

Then, just before entering the land, after a delay of forty years owing to Israel's disobedience and unbelief, Moses urged the people to keep God's commandments and added:

'For the Lord your God is bringing you into a good land, a land of brooks of water, of fountains and springs, flowing forth in valleys and hills, a land of wheat and barley, of vines and fig trees and pome-granates, a land of olive trees and honey, a land in which you will eat bread without scarcity, in which you will lack nothing, a land whose stones are iron, and out of whose hills you can dig copper. And you shall eat and be full, and you shall bless the Lord your God for the good land He has given you'.[11]

Although Palestinian farmers have to work hard to

secure a good yield, this is still an accurate description of the country's fertility and produce.

The country we are describing extends only about 200 miles from north to south and 100 miles from west to east. It is hemmed in by natural boundaries. To the north rises the mountainous mass of the Lebanon (meaning 'white' because of its snows) and the Anti-lebanon, the valley between being known as 'the entrance of Hamath'. To the west lies the Mediterranean or 'the Great Sea', and to the east and south the forbidding deserts of Arabia and of Zin.[12]

Several popular expressions were used to refer to the whole country from north to south. One was 'from the entrance of Hamath as far as the Sea of the Arabah', that is the Dead Sea.[13] But the commonest was simply 'from Dan to Beersheba',[14] Dan being Israel's most northerly city, while Beersheba was its most southerly, situated at the edge of the desert of Zin, about halfway between the Mediterranean and the southern tip of the Dead Sea.[15]

Visitors to the Holy Land, provided they have an opportunity to explore it adequately, are struck by the great variety of its terrain. The contrast is nowhere greater than between the 'seas' or 'lakes' at the northern and southern ends of the Jordan River. For the colourful beauty of Galilee—with its blue, mountain-girt lake, its carpet of springtime flowers and its distant backdrop of snow-capped Mount Hermon to the north—is a veritable paradise in comparison with the heat, the stench and the desolation of the Dead Sea and its environs.

The Biblical record often alludes to the different 'regions' into which Palestine is divided. For example, its inhabitants are described as living 'in the Arabah, in the hill country and in the lowland, and in the Negeb, and by the seacoast'.[16] The 'Arabah' is the deep gorge of the Jordan Valley running south to the Gulf of Aqabah.

The 'hillcountry' refers to the mountains of Judea, while the 'lowland' is the Shephelah, its western foothills. The 'Negeb', meaning 'the dry', is the great southern desert whose other name is the wilderness of Zin, and the 'seacoast' lies along the Mediterranean.

Perhaps a simpler way to remember the map of Palestine is to visualize four strips of country running parallel from north to south. The most striking is the Jordan valley. The river cuts its way deep between two mountain ranges—the central highlands which form the backbone of Palestine (its western slopes going down to the coastal plain) and the eastern tableland beyond which lies the desert. So the four strips between the sea and the desert are the coastland, the central highlands, the Jordan valley and the eastern tableland. We shall look at each in turn.

The Coastal Strip

The coastal strip varies in breadth from a few hundred yards where Mount Carmel juts out into the sea (and the modern port of Haifa is situated) to some thirty miles at the southern end. This southern part was the ancient land of the Philistines. It is here that the five main Philistine cities were located—Gaza the most southerly, on the great coastal road which runs up from Egypt about three miles inland, Ashkelon twelve miles north and on the sea, Ashdod eight miles farther north and on the road again, with Ekron farther north and more inland, and Gath in the middle of the plain.

The Shephelah or lowland lies immediately east of the Plain of Philistia. It is not surprising to read, therefore, that 'the Philistines . . . made raids on the cities in the Shephelah'.[17] Its sycamore trees were proverbial; so it could be said that Solomon 'made cedar as plentiful as the sycamore of the Shephelah'.[18] Its slopes are, in fact,

30

Palestine/
Coastal Strip

Central Highlands

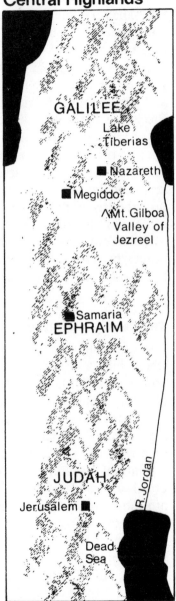

31

the foothills of the central plateau. They rise steadily from about 500 feet at Gath to 1,300 feet ten miles to the east. Then the mountains proper begin, and a further ten miles east lies Hebron, at 3,300 feet the highest city in Palestine.

Going back to the coast, immediately north of the plain of Philistia is the plain of Sharon, whose main town and port is Joppa. In our day it is rich in citrus orchards. Precisely what it was like in Biblical times is not certain, but it certainly supported flocks of sheep, since we read once or twice of 'the pasture lands of Sharon'.[19] On the other hand, before modern drainage it will have been very marshy, so that 'the majesty of ... Sharon'[20] probably refers to its luxuriant vegetation, and the 'rose of Sharon' (to whom the bride likens herself in the Song of Solomon) may have been an emblem of exceptional beauty because it blossomed in such unpromising surroundings, like 'a lily among brambles'.[21]

The Central Highlands

The central mountain range of Palestine begins in Galilee, whose hills and valleys were the background of Jesus' boyhood and of much of His public ministry. The peaks of Upper Galilee rise to just over 3000 feet, and from the hills above Nazareth in Lower Galilee, although not much higher than 1500 feet, the Mediterranean Sea is visible on a clear day only seventeen miles to the north-west.

South of Nazareth the ground slopes gently down to a broad alluvial plain, which runs in a south-easterly direction from the Mediterranean north of Mount Carmel to the River Jordan. Its western part is known as the Plain of Esdraelon; the eastern part is the narrower Valley of Jezreel, which lies between the formerly volcanic Hill of Moreh and the limestone Mount Gilboa. It was on the slopes of these two mountains that the

Philistines and the Israelites encamped, facing each other across the valley, before the final battle in which King Saul died:

'Now the Philistines fought against Israel; and the men of Israel fled before the Philistines, and fell slain on Mount Gilboa ... And David lamented with this lamentation over Saul and Jonathan his son ... "Thy glory, O Israel, is slain upon thy high places! How are the mighty fallen! ... Ye mountains of Gilboa, let there be no dew or rain upon you, nor upsurging of the deep! For there the shield of the mighty was defiled, the shield of Saul, not anointed with oil".'[22]

At the southern edge of the middle of the plain of Esdraelon, on a prominent site at the foot of the Carmel range, lies the fortress town of Megiddo. For centuries it has guarded the entrance to the main pass through the mountains to the south. It was one of the cities which King Solomon rebuilt and fortified to accommodate his horses and chariots[23]. Here also two kings of Judah died, Ahaziah who was shot by Jehu,[24] and Josiah who was killed while attempting to stop Pharaoh Neco of Egypt from going to the help of the Assyrians.[25]

South of the plain of Esdraelon lies the hill country of Manasseh and Ephraim, well covered with vineyards on their west-facing slopes, and still farther south the hill country of Judah. These two mountainous regions were the focal point of Israel's history during the period of the divided monarchy. For the capital of the northern kingdom was Samaria (in the land of Manesseh-Ephraim) and the capital of the southern kingdom was Jerusalem (in the land of Judah).

Jerusalem is built on a mountain surrounded by mountains. God's 'holy mountain, beautiful in elevation', the psalmist could sing, 'is the joy of all the earth.' Again, 'as the mountains are round about Jerusalem, so the Lord is round about His people'.[26] The Mount of Olives lies immediately to the east of Jerusalem, across the Kidron valley, and from this summit the road runs east through the most barren land imaginable, dropping more than 3000 feet to Jericho and on to the Dead Sea. It was while making this two-day journey on foot that the traveller in Christ's parable was attacked by brigands and rescued by the Good Samaritan.

The whole area between Jerusalem and the Dead Sea is known as the Wilderness of Judea, and it was somewhere in this scene of desolation that Jesus spent forty days following His baptism, fasting and being tempted by the devil.

The Jordan Valley

The Jordan Valley is part of the Great Rift Valley which stretches for 4,000 miles from Asia Minor through the Red Sea to the Rift Valley lakes of East Africa. But the River Jordan itself is only about eighty miles in total length, excluding its meanderings. It rises in Mount Hermon, a 9,000 feet shoulder of the Antilebanon mass, and then maintains a steady descent ('Jordan' means 'descender') through Lake Huleh and Lake Tiberias until it peters out in the Dead Sea. At Huleh it is still above sea level (about 230 feet), but Lake Tiberias is nearly 700 feet below, while its final descent takes it to about 1,300 feet below at the Dead Sea, whose bottom at over 2,500 feet is the deepest point on the surface of the earth.

Lake Huleh is known in the Bible as 'the waters of Merom' but does not feature prominently in the Biblical narrative.[27] It has always been the haunt rather of birds than of men—Purple Herons still nest in its tall papyrus reeds—although recently most of it was drained for agricultural land.

Lake Tiberias is called in the Gospels sometimes 'the

Palestine/
Jordan Valley

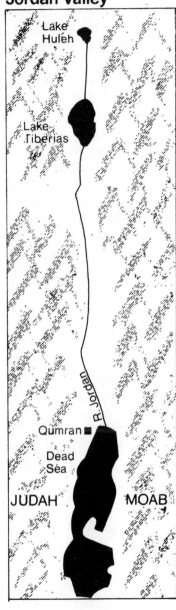

Eastern Tableland

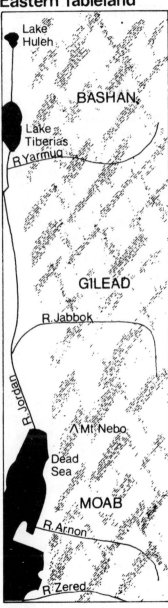

35

Sea of Chinnereth' (or Gennesaret) but usually 'the Sea of Galilee', although to Luke the much-travelled evangelist who knew the Mediterranean first-hand it is always merely a 'lake'[28]. Indeed, he is right, for it is only twelve miles long and—at its widest point—only seven miles across. It is deep and full of fish, and the first disciples of Jesus, the two pairs of brothers, Andrew and Simon, James and John, were partners in a fishing business on the lake. Although the lake is almost surrounded by mountains, there were numerous villages round its northern and western shores, and these Jesus visited when He went about preaching, teaching and healing.

South of Lake Tiberias the Jordan river flows for a further 65 miles (though the mileage is more like 200 if all the meanderings are included) until it reaches the Dead Sea. For much of this distance it is unimpressive and muddy, so that one has some sympathy for Naaman the leprous Syrian general who had no desire to be cured by having to wash in it:

'Are not Abana and Pharpar, the rivers of Damascus, better than all the waters of Israel? Could I not wash in them and be clean?'[29]

More impressive was the thick jungle of the river valley, a famous haunt of wild animals, so that God could liken Himself in His judgments to 'a lion coming up from the jungle of the Jordan against a strong sheepfold'.[30]

The exact site of the baptisms administered by John the Baptist is unknown, but it must have been at one of the fords a few miles from where the Jordan enters the Dead Sea. Thus:

'There went out to him all the country of Judea, and all the people of Jerusalem; and they were baptized by him in the river Jordan, confessing their sins'.[31]

The whole of the Palestinian Rift Valley is called in the Old Testament 'the Arabah', meaning 'dry', and the

Dead Sea is 'the Sea of the Arabah' or 'the Salt Sea'. This is forty-eight miles long and a scene of almost unrelieved desolation. Its eastern shore is overlooked by the sheer cliffs of the mountains of Moab, while on the west are the barren slopes of the mountains of Judah. Here (at Qumran) lived the Essene monastic community before and during the time of Christ, and here in our time the Dead Sea Scrolls were found in some of the caves which honeycomb the hills.

The heat is so intense (up to 110° in the summer), the evaporation so great and the rainfall so small, that the water level of the Dead Sea remains constant despite the inflowing streams and the absence of all outflow. As a result, the chemical deposits in the water (especially salt, potash and magnesium) are highly concentrated, and no fish can survive.[32] It seems likely that Sodom and Gomorrah, 'the cities of the plain', were situated in the area now covered by the southern tip of the Dead Sea. And it is not impossible that the 'brimstone and fire' which the Lord 'rained' on them, together with the 'pillar of salt' into which Lot's wife was changed, were the results of an earthquake and eruption which God used to destroy them for their wickedness.[33]

The Arabah continues south of the Dead Sea until it reaches the Red Sea at the Gulf of Aqabah. Here was the port of Ezion Geber (the equivalent of the modern Elath), giving Israel access by sea to the trade of Africa and Asia. For 'King Solomon built a fleet of ships at Ezion-Geber . . .'.[34] Copper was exported from the nearby mines which Solomon developed, while imports included such exotic items as 'gold, silver, ivory, apes and peacocks'.[35]

The Eastern Tableland

The fourth strip of Palestinian country we have to consider is the eastern tableland, between the Jordan Valley and the Arabian desert. This was the area inherited by two and a half of Israel's twelve tribes:

> 'Gad and Reuben and half the tribe of Manasseh . . . received their inheritance beyond the Jordan eastward'.[36]

It is a vast plateau stretching for about 250 miles from north to south, divided by four rivers which have cut deep canyons on their way westwards into the River Jordan or the Dead Sea. The first is the River Yarmuq, which flows into the Jordan just south of Lake Tiberias. The second is the River Jabbok which reaches the Jordan approximately half way between Lake Tiberias and the Dead Sea. It was here that 'Jacob was left alone, and a man wrestled with him until the breaking of the. day'.[37] The River Arnon flows into the middle of the Dead Sea and the River Zered into its southern tip. These rivers formed natural frontiers for Israel's neighbouring tribes, Ammon claiming the territory between the Jabbok and the Arnon, Moab that between the Arnon and the Zered (though often spilling over to the north), and Edom that south of the Zered.

Perhaps it is easiest, however, to visualize the plateau east of the Jordan by remembering the main divisions which Denis Baly describes in his *The Geography of the Bible*.[38] Bashan, the tableland east of Lake Tiberias, he calls 'the land of the farmer', for though it was probably well wooded in Bible times it was famed for its corn crop and for its rams, lambs, goats and bulls, 'all of them fatlings of Bashan'.[39]

South of Bashan was Gilead, a term covering virtually the whole of Transjordan between Lake Tiberias and the Dead Sea. This is 'the land of the highlander'. As the terrain rises to over 3,000 feet, the rainfall is considerable and brings fertility to both forest and vineyard. The grapes of Gilead were unrivalled throughout Palestine and 'the balm of Gilead' (an aromatic spice of some kind) was famous. The caravan of Ishmaelites to whom Joseph was sold by his brothers were 'coming from Gilead, with their camels bearing gum, balm and myrrh, on their way to carry it down to Egypt'.[40]

Continuing our journey south in Transjordan, Moab comes next, occupying the mountainous territory east of the Dead Sea. Apart from the deep gorges of the river Arnon and of some smaller streams, most of Moab is a high plateau. Denis Baly calls it 'the land of the shepherd':

'Everywhere . . . there are sheep, great flocks and converging lines of them, like the spokes of a limitless wheel, moving in clouds of golden dust to be given their water at the well'.[41]

So too we read in the Bible:

'Now Mesha King of Moab was a sheep breeder; and he had to deliver annually to the King of Israel a hundred thousand lambs, and the wool of a hundred thousand rams'.[42]

It was from the mountains of Moab (Mt. Nebo, to be precise) that Moses viewed the promised land before he died, and on the plains of Moab that the children of Israel encamped before crossing the Jordan to take possession of it.[43]

The most southerly section of Transjordan is Edom. At its highest points it rises to about 3,500 feet, towering above the deserts to the west, east and south. Denis Baly names it 'the land of the trader', for through it passed the great eastern trade route known as 'the King's Highway'. It was because of Edom's refusal to allow Israel to use this route on their way to the promised land that there was long-standing enmity between the two countries.[44]

Such is the 'good land' which the Lord their God gave to Israel. It was a country for farmers, who kept livestock and cultivated the arable land.

39

Agriculture and Rainfall

Their livestock consisted mostly of sheep and goats, which roamed in huge mixed flocks over the hills and the steppe. The goats supplied milk and the black hair of which Bedouin tents were made, while the sheep gave milk, meat and wool. Because Palestinian shepherds kept their sheep more for wool than for mutton, however, quite an intimate relationship grew up between them over the years. The shepherd would lead his sheep, not drive them. He would know them individually, and call them by name, while they for their part would know his voice and follow him. It seemed only natural that God should reveal Himself as the 'Shepherd of Israel' who would 'gather the lambs in His arms, . . . carry them in His bosom, and gently lead those that are with young',[45] and indeed that the godly Israelite should be able to affirm:

'The Lord is my shepherd, I shall not want; He makes me lie down in green pastures. He leads me beside still waters'.[46]

The Lord Jesus developed the metaphor further, calling Himself 'the Good Shepherd' and affirming that He would both lay down His life for the sheep and go out into the desert in search of only one that was lost.[47]

Though many Israelite farmers kept livestock, even more cultivated the soil. The three main products of Palestine are bracketed together in many Biblical passages. Before they entered the land, this was the reward which they were promised for their obedience:

'The Lord your God . . . will . . . bless . . . the fruit of your ground, your grain and your wine and your oil.'

When they had taken possession of it, they proved God's faithfulness in giving 'wine to gladden the heart of man, oil to make his face shine, and bread to strengthen man's heart'. But when they rebelled against Him He witheld these blessings—through famine or pestilence or locusts—until they repented and He could say to them:

'Behold, I am sending to you grain, wine and oil, and you will be satisfied'.[48]

The grain from which their bread came was mostly wheat and barley,while the wine came from the extensive vineyards, and the oil (principally for cooking) from the olive-yards. Olive trees are particularly hardy, being able to survive in shallow soil and to withstand long periods of drought.

Other fruits of ancient Israel were pomegranates, and especially figs, so that the sweetest Israelite dream of peace and security in the Messianic kingdom was:

'they shall sit every man under his vine and under his fig tree, and none shall make them afraid'.[49]

For a good harvest the land was entirely dependent upon rain. The Israelite knew that there was no greater blessing of God. It was 'the living God who made the heaven and the earth and the sea and all that is in them' who gave 'from heaven rains and fruitful seasons', thus bearing witness to His own faithfulness. And so great is His grace to all mankind, Jesus emphasized, that 'He makes His sun rise on the evil and on the good, and sends rain on the just and on the unjust'.[50]

Generally speaking, the Palestinian rainy seasons are predictable. The summer extends from May/June to September/October, and during these five months rain is virtually unknown, so that Samuel's prayer for rain during wheat harvest was a request for a miracle. Indeed, 'snow in summer or rain in harvest' is as out of place as 'honour . . . for a fool'.[51] During this dry season there is only the dew to bring moisture, and the morning mist. But both dissipate speedily when the sun rises, and their disappearance is used as a picture of idolatrous Israel when the judgment of God falls:

'They shall be like the morning mist or like the dew that goes early away'.[52]

From about mid-October, however, the rain clouds begin to form, and when the rain finally comes, often accompanied by thunder, there is nothing to do but run for shelter. Denis Baly describes the scene:

'Jesus quoted it as a well-known occurrence that a badly built house might collapse during the rainy season (Mt. 7.27) and, indeed, it is only when one has seen a storm sweeping in from the Mediterranean across the Palestinian hills or the torrents pouring down the precipitous slopes into the lake of Galilee that one knows quite what a concentrated fury is contained in those words, "and the rain fell, and the floods came, and the winds blew and beat against that house".'[53]

The beginning of the rainy season was usually termed 'the early rains', and, far from being regarded as destructive, they were looked upon as beneficial, indeed indispensable. Without them ploughing was impossible, for the sun-baked earth was hard as iron.[54] But once the rains had started and begun to soften the soil, especially if their arrival was late, the farmer must brave the weather and get on with his ploughing if he was to be able to sow his fields in time for harvest. Jesus used this as a picture of Christian courage and perseverance:

'No one who puts his hand to the plough and looks back is fit for the kingdom of God'.[55]

If the 'early rains' at the start of the rainy season (from November) were essential to ploughing, the 'latter rains' at its end (in March and April) were essential to reaping. Without them the corn would remain thin and desiccated; it was the rain which swelled and matured the grain for the harvest. And when the fields were finally 'white for harvest', the labourers would put in their sickles.[56] The corn would then be tied into sheaves and carted by donkeys or camels to the threshing floor, a flat hardened surface at the top of a local hillock. There it would be first threshed by animal hooves or a sledge[57] and afterwards winnowed. Tossed into the air with a pitch fork, the precious golden grain would fall to the earth to be garnered, while the wind would blow the chaff away. This separation of wheat from chaff became a common image for the divine judgment.[58]

So 'the early and the latter rain', sometimes called 'the autumn rain and the spring rain',[59] were a necessary prelude to a good harvest. God had Himself linked the rain and the harvest together and promised them to His obedient people:

'If you will obey My commandments which I command you this day, to love the Lord your God, and to serve Him with all your heart and with all your soul, He will give the rain for your land in its season, the early rain and the later rain, that you may gather in your grain and your wine and your oil'.[60]

Wise farmers knew this and waited for 'the precious fruit' of the earth, being patient over it until it receives the early and the late rain'.[61] Consequently, when the rains were given they were full of thanksgiving to God for His mercy. No more poetic account of His harvest blessings occurs in Scripture than in Psalm 65. Notice the reference both to the early rains which water the hard ground, 'settling its ridges, softening it with showers', and to the 'crown' of the year some eight months later when 'the valleys deck themselves with grain':

'Thou visitest the earth and waterest it, Thou greatly enrichest it; the river of God is full of water; thou providest their grain, for so Thou hast prepared it. Thou waterest its furrows abundantly, settling its ridges, softening it with showers, and blessing its growth. Thou crownest the year with Thy bounty; the tracks of Thy chariot drip with fatness. The pastures of the wilderness drip, the hills gird themselves with joy, the meadows clothe themselves with flocks, the valleys deck themselves with grain, they shout and sing together for joy.'[62]

The Three Annual Festivals

In the light of Israel's closeness to the soil as a farming community, it is not surprising that their three annual festivals had an agricultural as well as a religious significance. In them they worshipped the God of nature and the God of grace as the one God, Lord of the earth and of Israel.

The Feast of the Passover, followed immediately by the Feast of Unleavened Bread, commemorated primarily Israel's redemption from Egypt. But it also took place about the middle of April when the first sheaf of ripe barley could be waved humbly and gratefully before the Lord.

The second was the Feast of the Firstfruits or Harvest, also called the Feast of Weeks or Pentecost because it was celebrated seven weeks or fifty days after the Passover, that is, at about the beginning of June. It was a thanksgiving for the completed grain harvest—wheat as well as barley. Later it came to be regarded also as commemorating the giving of the law at Mt. Sinai, perhaps because in connection with it Israel was told:

'You shall remember that you were a slave in Egypt;

44

and you shall be careful to observe these statutes'.[63]

The last of the three annual festivals was the Feast of Booths or Tabernacles. For seven days the people had to dwell in booths made out of tree branches. God's purpose in requiring this was clear:

'that your generation may know that I made the people of Israel dwell in booths when I brought them out of the land of Egypt'.[64]

But this festival was also known as the Feast of Ingathering, for it took place in mid-October, six months later than the Passover, by which time each year the produce of vineyard and oliveyard as well as grainfield had been gathered in.

The observance of these three annual festivals was obligatory. God had said:

'Three times in the year you shall keep a feast to Me. You shall keep the feast of unleavened bread . . . You shall keep the feast of harvest, of the first fruits of your labour, of what you sow in the field. You shall keep the feast of ingathering at the end of the year, when you gather in from the field the fruit of your labour'.[65]

From one point of view these festivals commemorated the signal mercies of the covenant God of Israel who first redeemed His people from their Egyptian bondage, then gave them the law at Sinai and then provided for them during their wanderings in the wilderness. From another point of view the three feasts were all harvest festivals, marking respectively the beginning of the barley harvest, the end of the grain harvest, and the end of the fruit harvest.

So Israel was taught to honour Jehovah both as God of creation and as God of salvation. The two themes were brought together in what the people of Israel were to do when they had come into the land of promise:

'You shall take some of the first of all the fruit of the ground, . . . put it in a basket, . . . go to the priest . . . and say to him, "I declare this day to the Lord your God that I have come into the land which the Lord swore to our fathers to give us. . . . And behold, now I bring the first of the fruit of the ground, which Thou, O Lord, hast given me" . . . and you shall rejoice in all the good which the Lord your God has given to you . . .'.[66]

Here was rich symbolism indeed. The basket of fruit was a token of 'all the good' which God had given Israel. It was the fruit of the ground, fruit which God had caused to grow. But from what ground? From ground which God had also given them, as He had sworn to their fathers. The fruit was a sacrament of both creation and redemption, for it was the fruit of the promised land.

For Further Reading

The Geography of the Bible by Denis Baly (Lutterworth 1957, 303 pages). A descriptive survey of the whole of Palestine, both general and regional, by one who lived in the country for 15 years. Well illustrated by the author's own maps, charts and black-and-white photographs.

Oxford Bible Atlas (2nd edition) by H. G. May (Oxford 1974, 144 pages). The Oxford Bible Atlas is a competent and reasonably priced guide to every aspect of the geographical background of the Bible. It includes descriptive texts as well as maps.

The Way It Was in Bible Times by Merrill T. Gilbertson (Augsburg 1959, Lutterworth 1961, 142 pages). A short, simple book by a Lutheran pastor on the cultural background of the Bible. There are chapters on Israelite homes, food and clothing, social and religious customs, occupations, measurements and education, illustrated by black-and-white drawings.

NOTES

1 Rom. 15.4; 1 Cor. 10.11
2 Rom. 15.4
3 This expression is used with regard both to an Old Testament prophet like Elijah and to a New Testament apostle like Paul. See Jas. 5.17 and Acts 14.15
4 1 Cor. 10.6, 11
5 Acts 1.8
6 Ezek. 5.5
7 Ex. 3.8
8 Ezek. 20.6, 15
9 Num. 14.6–8
10 Num. 13.23, 24
11 Deut. 8.7–10
12 These boundaries are described in Num. 34.1–15
13 e.g. 2 Kings 14.25
14 e.g. Judges 20.1; 1 Sam. 3.20; 2 Sam. 3.10; 1 Kings 4.25
15 It was to Beersheba that the prophet Elijah fled when his life was threatened by Queen Jezebel. See 1 Kings 19.1–3
16 Deut. 1.7
17 2 Chron. 28.18
18 1 Kings 10.27
19 1 Chron. 5.16 cf. 27.29
20 Is. 35.2
21 Song of Solomon 2.1, 2
22 1 Sam. 31.1; 2 Sam. 1.17, 19, 21
23 1 Kings 9.15, 19
24 2 Kings 9.27
25 2 Chron. 35.20–24 cf. 2 Kings 23.28–30
26 Ps. 48.1, 2; 125.2
27 In fact, only in Josh. 11.5, 7
28 For 'Chinnereth' see Num. 34.11 and Deut. 3.17; for 'Gennesaret' Lk. 5.1
29 2 Kings 5.12
30 Jer. 49.19
31 Mk. 1.5
32 cf. Ezek. 47.1–12
33 Gen. 19.24–29
34 1 Kings 9.26
35 1 Kings 10.22 cf. v.11
36 Josh. 18.7
37 Gen. 32.22–32
38 pp. 217–251
39 Ezek. 39.18 cf. Ps. 22.12
40 Gen. 37.25 cf. Jer. 8.22
41 p. 237
42 2 Kings 3.4
43 Deut. 32.49, 50; 34.1–8; Num. 22.1
44 Num. 20.14–21; 21.4
45 Ps. 80.1; Is. 40.11
46 Ps. 23.1, 2
47 John 10.1–18; Lk. 15.3–7
48 Deut. 7.13; Ps. 104.15; Joel 2.19 cf. Hos. 2.8
49 Mic. 4.4

50 Acts 14. 15–17; Mt. 5.45
51 1 Sam. 12.16–18; Prov. 26.1
52 Hos. 13.3
53 p. 79
54 Deut. 28.23
55 Lk. 9.62
56 Jn. 4.35; Joel 3.13
57 cf. Is. 41.15
58 e.g. Ps. 1.4; Lk. 3.17
59 Jer. 5.24
60 Deut. 11.13, 14
61 Jas. 5.7
62 Ps. 65.9–13
63 Deut. 16.12
64 Lev. 23.39–43
65 Ex. 23.14–17 cf. Deut. 16.16, 17
66 Deut. 26.1–11

Have you seen
The Scripture Union
KEY BOOKS
Range?

UNDERSTANDING CHRISTIAN ATTITUDES
George Hoffman

The author deals positively and clearly with the Christian approach to a wide number of social and moral problems.

UNDERSTANDING THE SUPERNATURAL
Canon Stafford Wright

A timely assessment of the occult based on the warnings given in the Bible and the Christian's understanding of the power of Christ and the nature of evil.

UNDERSTANDING THE TEN COMMANDMENTS
John Eddison

The author considers the relevance of the Ten Commandments to contemporary life.

UNDERSTANDING OURSELVES
John Eddison

A sympathetic, Christian view of the anxiety and depression that trouble so many in today's world.

UNDERSTANDING THE WAY
Robinson and Winward

A practical guide to the Christian life.

UNDERSTANDING CHRISTIAN ETHICS
Gilbert Kirby

The principal of the London Bible College considers the application of Christian teaching in dealing with contemporary problems from euthanasia to pornography.

UNDERSTANDING BASIC BELIEFS
John Eddison

An outline of what Christians believe based on one of the great creeds of the Christian church.

LET'S TALK IT THROUGH
J. Hills Cotterill

Discussion starters and background material on a variety of topics from contemporary portrayals of Jesus Christ to the use of music in worship. A mine of information.

UNDERSTANDING LEADERSHIP
John Eddison

Ten studies on 'top men' of the Bible which aim to show exactly what the qualities are that make up a leader.

UNDERSTANDING GOD'S PLAN
David Howard

A very readable commentary on the great themes of the book of Job and their message for us in today's world.

UNDERSTANDING THE DEATH OF JESUS
John Eddison

A lively challenging look at the reasons why Jesus died on the cross and the implications of his death for us today.

UNDERSTANDING THE CHRISTIAN AND SEX
M. O. Vincent

A trained psychiatrist explores the role of sex in the life of the world and of the individual Christian.

DAILY BIBLE STUDY BOOKS

Thorough coverage of major Biblical passages combines scholarly insight with devotional warmth and practical experience. Studies of Biblical characters are also included.

Man separated from God   A. Skevington Wood
E. M. Blaiklock

Jesus' Early Life   H. L. Ellison
E. M. Blaiklock

Jesus' True Identity   James Philip
E. M. Blaiklock

Man restored in Christ   W. L. Lane
E. M. Blaiklock

God the Holy Spirit   Leon Morris
E. M. Blaiklock

Christ Living with Him   J. I. Packer
E. M. Blaiklock

God's Kingdom and Church   F. F. Bruce
E. M. Blaiklock

Christ the Way to God   R. A. Finlayson
E. M. Blaiklock

UNDERSTANDING THE NEW TESTAMENT

Based on Scripture Union's popular *Daily Bible Commentary* in four volumes these ten books offer a unique combination of daily Bible readings with the depth of a commentary.

St Matthew   F. F. Bruce

St Mark   I. H. Marshall

St Luke   E. M. Blaiklock

St John   R. E. Nixon

Acts   R. P. Martin

Romans   E. M. Blaiklock

1 Corinthians—Galatians   R. P.Martin

Ephesians—2 Thessalonians   W. L. Lane

1 Timothy—James   Leon Morris

1 Peter—Revelation   H. L. Ellison

SCRIPTURE UNION BIBLE DICTIONARIES

DICTIONARY OF BIBLE WORDS
John Eddison

John Eddison looks at a range of Bible words that are unfamiliar in everyday English and explains their original meaning and modern significance.

DICTIONARY OF BIBLE TIMES
Herbert Sundemo

With the help of maps, charts and over 200 line drawings the author covers, in one handy volume, topics ranging from geography to religious customs.

DICTIONARY OF BIBLE PEOPLE
J. Stafford Wright

Over 500 entries covering the major characters in the Bible. All the relevant facts of their lives are detailed and discussed in a lively, memorable style.

Your Own Personal Notes

Your Own Personal Notes

Your Own Personal Notes